CELTIC DESIGN

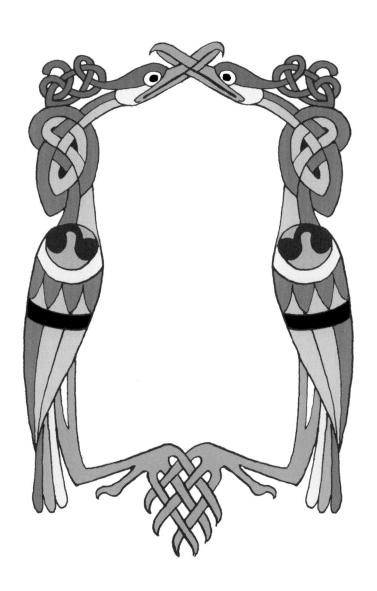

CELTIC DESIGN

DOVERPICTURA

DOVER PUBLICATIONS, INC. | Mineola, New York

Selected and designed by Althea Chen, Faith Brosnan, and Alan Weller.

Celtic Design is a new work, first published by Dover Publications, Inc., in 2007.

For permission to use more than ten images, please contact:
Permissions Department
Dover Publications, Inc.
31 East 2nd Street
Mineola, NY 11501
rights@doverpublications.com

The CD-ROM file names correspond to the images in the book. All of the artwork stored on the CD-ROM can be imported directly into a wide range of design and word-processing programs on either Windows or Macintosh platforms. No further installation is necessary.

International Standard Book Number: 0-486-99799-5

Manufactured in the United States of America
Dover Publications, Inc., 31 East 2nd Street, Mineola, NY 11501
www.doverpublications.com

004

005

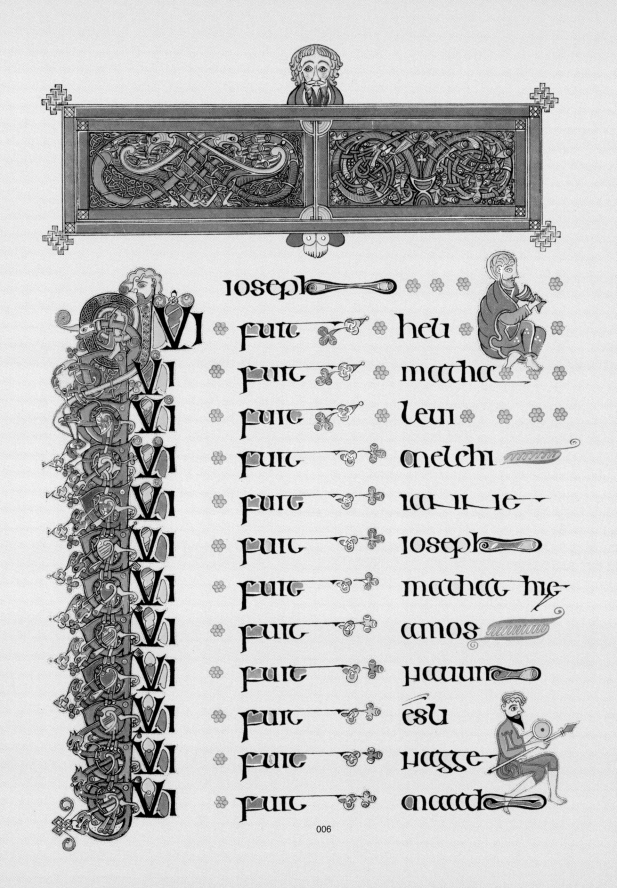

ioseph

VI fuit heli

VI fuit macha

VI fuit leui

VI fuit melchi

VI fuit ianne

VI fuit ioseph

VI fuit mathat hie

VI fuit amos

VI fuit naum

VI fuit esli

VI fuit hagge

VI fuit maath

006

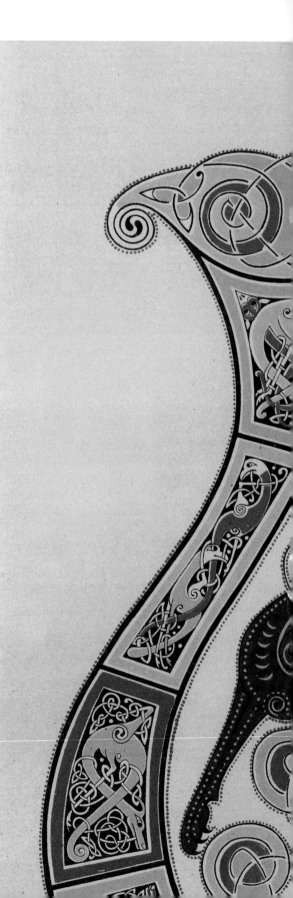

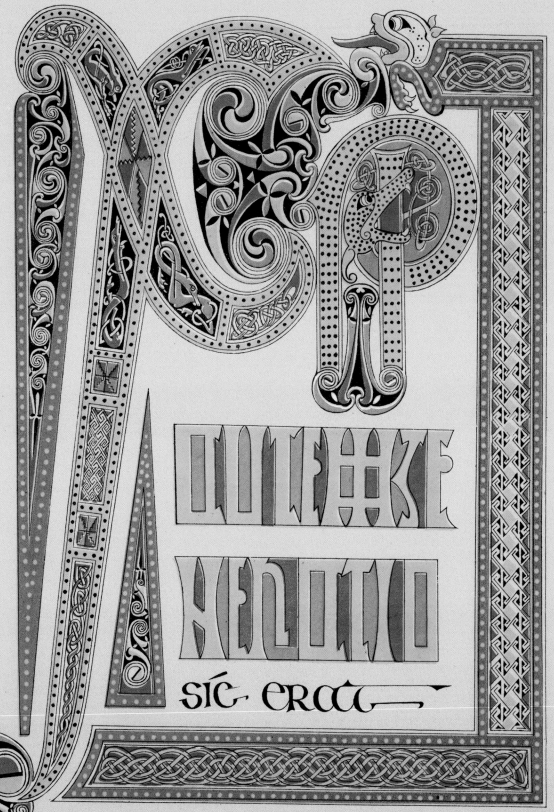

XPI OUIEHKE HENOTIO
síc eRat

010

011

012

014

016

017

018

Io han nis.

022

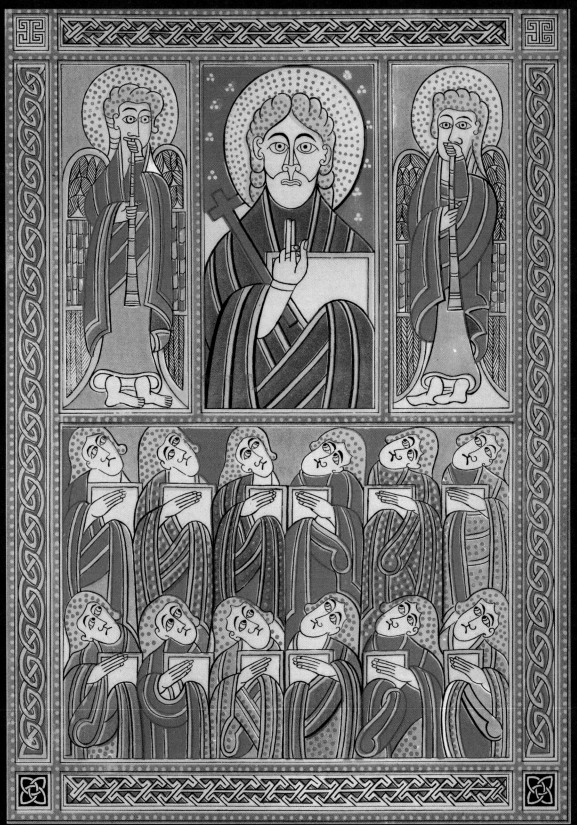

hGENERATIO

033

034

035

036

037

038

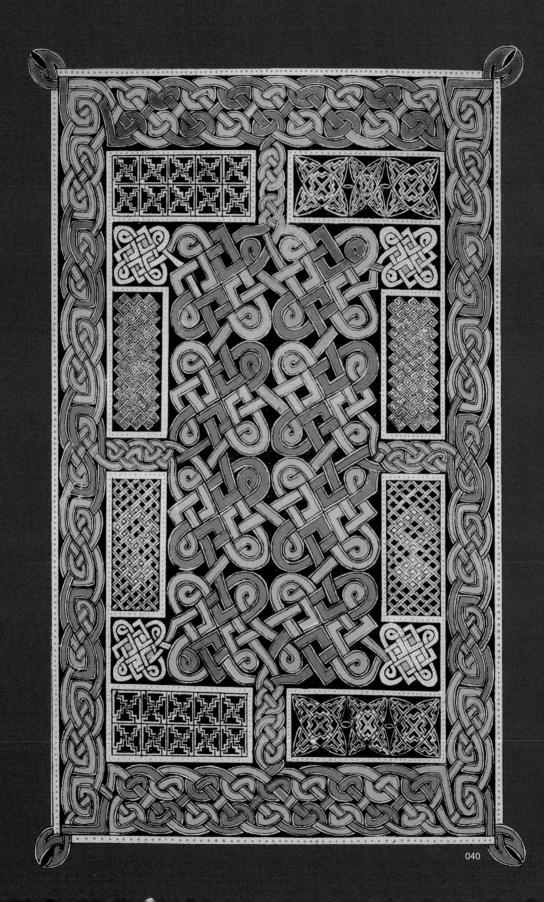

041

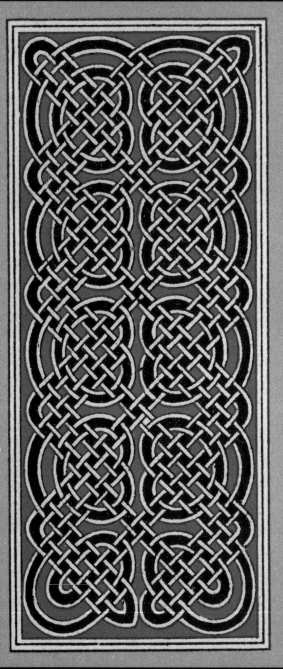

044

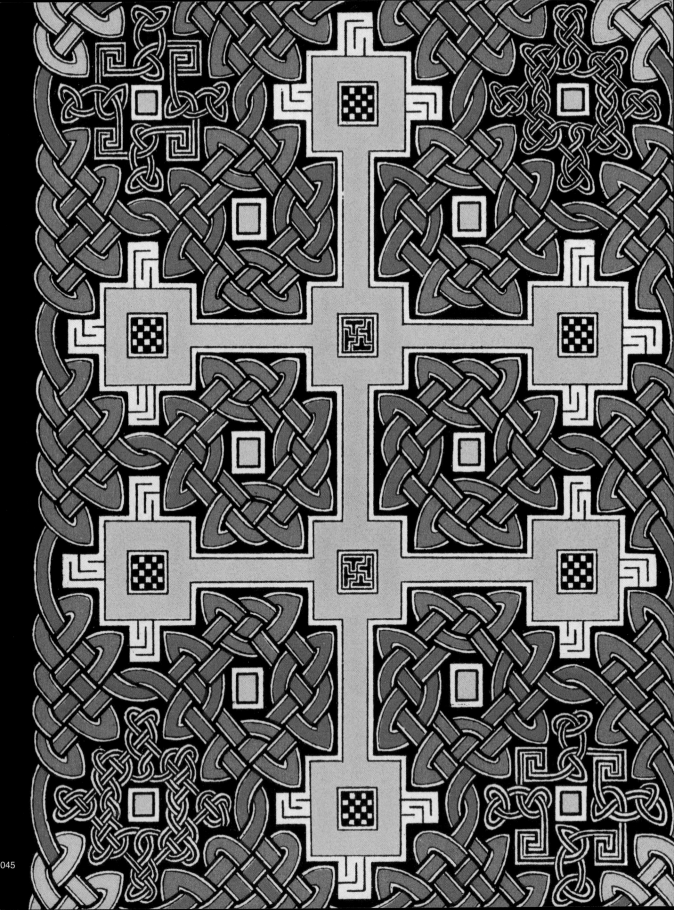

046

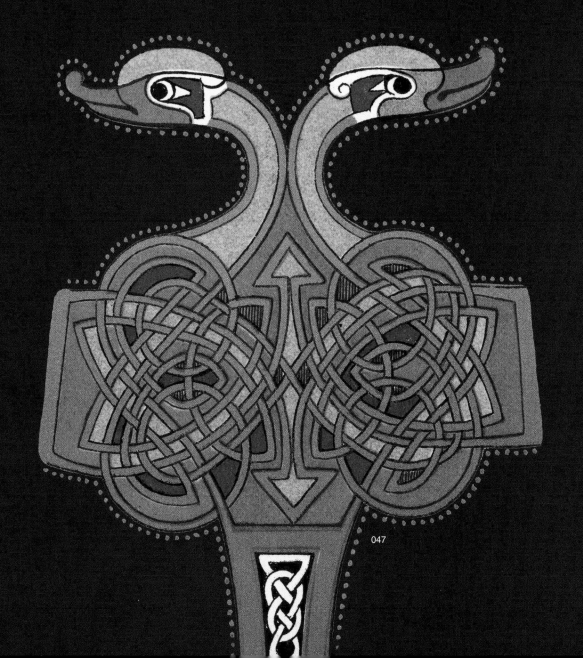

047

048

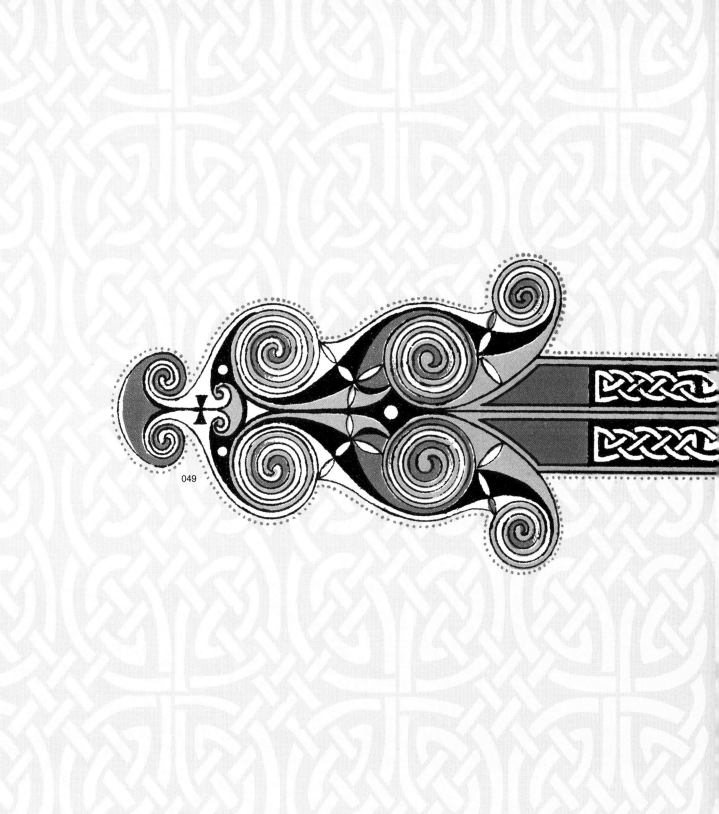

049

050

051

052

053

056

058

060

059

061

062

063

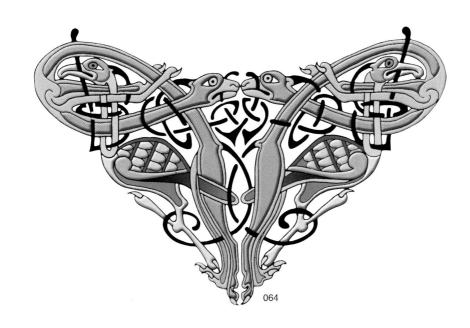

064

065

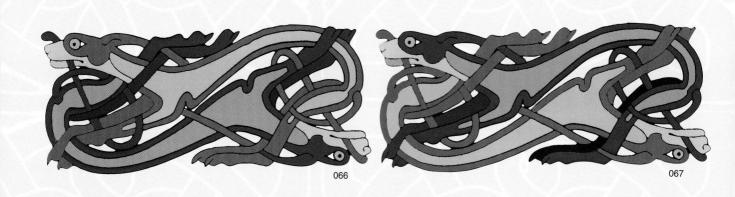

066

067

068

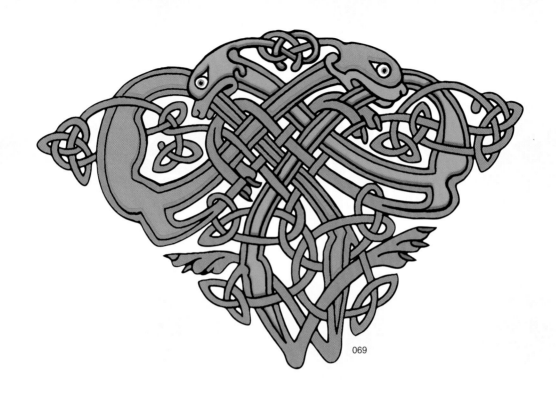

069

070

071

072

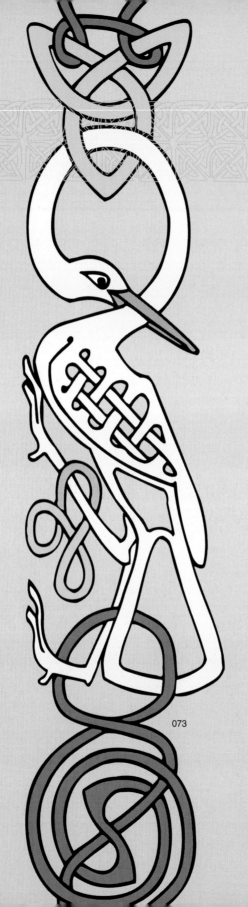

073

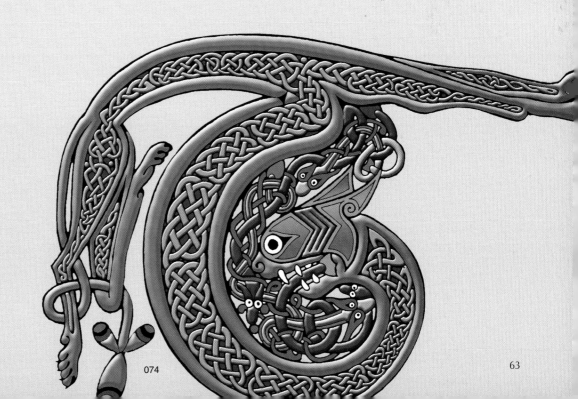

075

077

078

079

080

081

082

083

084

085

086

087

088

089

090

091

092

093

094

095

097

096

098

099

100

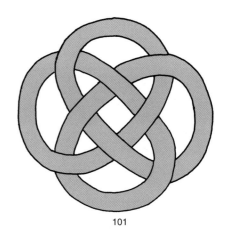

101

102

103

104

105

106

107

108

109

110

111   112   113   114

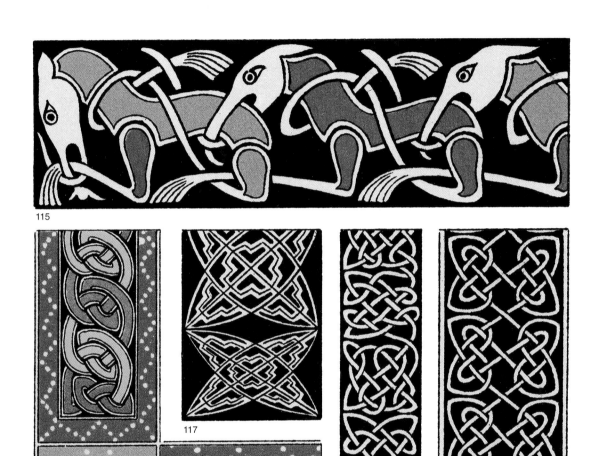

115

116

117

118 119

120

121

122

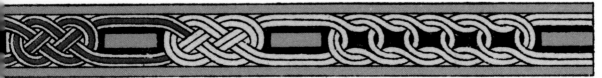

123

124

125

126

127

128

129 130 131

132

133

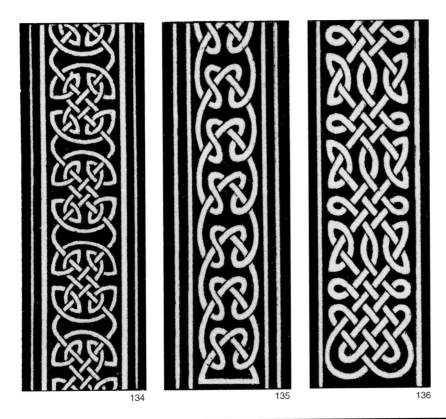

134   135   136

137

138

139

140

141

142

143

144

145

146

147

148

149

150

151

152

153

154

155

156

157

158

159

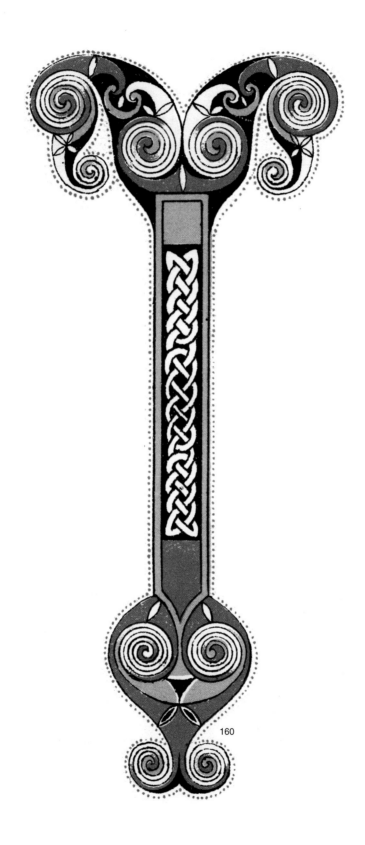

160

161

162

163

164

165

166

167

94

168

169

170

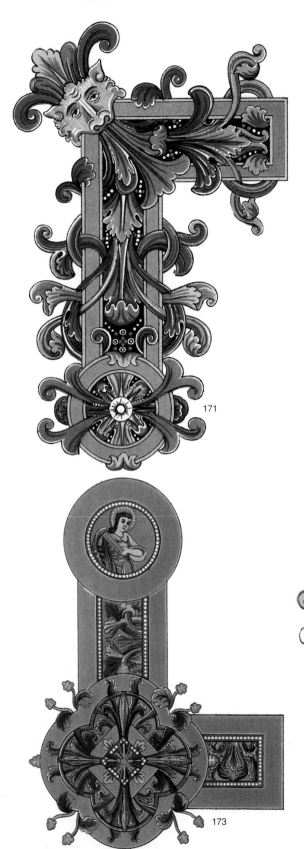

171

173

172

174

175

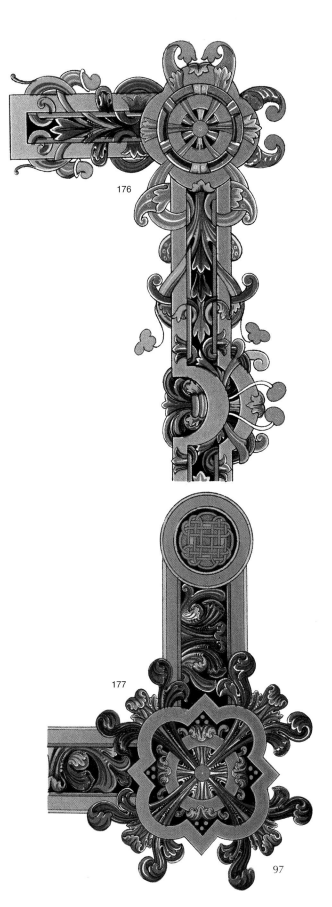

176

177

97

179

180

181

182

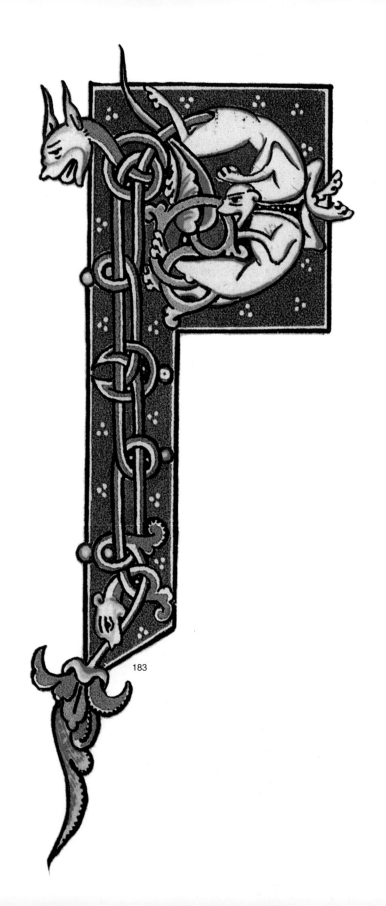

183

184

185

186

187

188

190

191

192

193

194

195

196

197

198

109

199

200

201

202

203

204

205

206

207

208

209

210

211

212

111

213

214

215

216

217

218

219

220

221

223

222

225

224

226

227

228

229

232

231

230

233

234

235

236

237

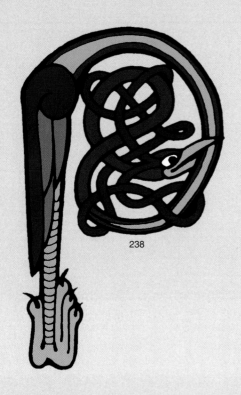

238

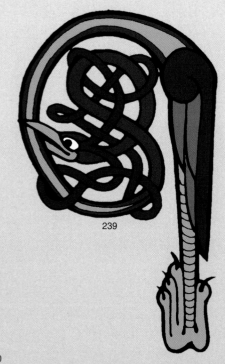

239

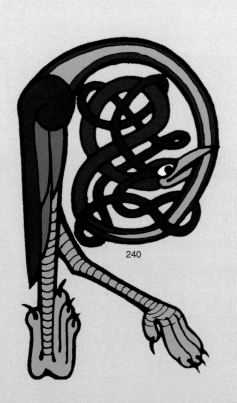

240

241

242

243

244

245

246

247

248

249

250

251

252

253

254

255

257

256

258

259

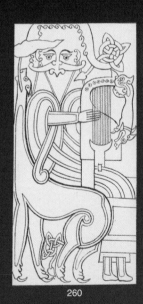

260

261

262   263   264   265   266

267   268

269   270   271